Celebrations

Let's Get Ready for Passover

By Lloyd G. Douglas

Children's Press®
A Division of Scholastic Inc.
New York / Toronto / London / Auckland / Sydney
Mexico City / New Delhi / Hong Kong
Danbury, Connecticut

Photo Credits: Cover and all photos by Maura B. McConnell except p. 7 © Bettmann/CORBIS
Contributing Editor: Jennifer Silate
Book Design: Christopher Logan

Library of Congress Cataloging-in-Publication Data

Douglas, Lloyd G.
  Let's get ready for Passover / by Lloyd G. Douglas.
  p. cm. — (Celebrations)
  Includes index.
  Summary: A simple introduction to a family's celebration of Passover.
  ISBN 0-516-24260-1 (lib. bdg.) — ISBN 0-516-24352-7 (pbk.)
  1. Passover—Juvenile literature. [1. Passover. 2. Holidays.] I.
  Title. II. Celebrations (Children's Press)

BM695.P3 D68 2003
296.4'37—dc21

                                              2002008183

Contents

1 Getting Ready
for Passover   4

2 Setting the Table   8

3 Celebrating Passover   16

4 New Words   22

5 To Find Out More   23

6 Index   24

7 About the Author   24

My name is Joel.

Tonight is the first night of **Passover**.

My parents and I are getting ready.

5

Long ago, **Jewish** people were **slaves** in a country called **Egypt**.

During Passover, we **celebrate** when the Jewish people became **free**.

Passover lasts for eight days.

6

We use special plates during Passover.

I help set the plates on the table.

9

I also help put the food on the table.

The food we eat during Passover helps us to remember the Jewish slaves.

This is **matzoh**.

Matzoh is flat, hard bread.

Jewish people ate matzoh after they left Egypt.

We eat many other different foods during Passover, too.

They each have a special meaning.

15

My grandparents come to our house for dinner.

We sit around the table.

It is time for us to celebrate Passover.

We read a story about the Jewish slaves who became free long ago.

We eat food at special times during the story.

The first night of Passover is finished.

Happy Passover!

New Words

celebrate (**sel**-uh-brate) to do something enjoyable on a special occasion

Egypt (**ee**-jipt) a country in Africa

free (**free**) going where you want or doing what you want

Jewish (**joo**-ish) someone whose family comes from the ancient Hebrew tribes of Israel

matzoh (**mat**-zuh) flat, hard bread

Passover (**pass**-oh-vur) an important Jewish holiday celebrating when the Jews escaped from slavery in Egypt

slaves (**slayvz**) people who are owned by other people and thought of as property

To Find Out More

Books
On Passover
by Cathy Goldberg Fishman
Atheneum

Passover
by David F. Marx
Children's Press

Web Site
Passover at Kids Domain
http://www.kidsdomain.com/holiday/passover/
Find out how to do fun Passover crafts, send your friends a
Passover e-card, and learn about Passover on this Web site.

Index

celebrate, 6, 16

dinner, 16

Egypt, 6, 12

food, 10, 14, 18

matzoh, 12

Passover, 4, 6,
    8, 10, 14,
    16, 20

remember, 10

slaves, 6, 10, 18
story, 18

About the Author
Lloyd G. Douglas is an editor and writer of children's books.

Reading Consultants
Kris Flynn, Coordinator, Small School District Literacy, The San Diego County
    Office of Education

Shelly Forys, Certified Reading Recovery Specialist, W.J. Zahnow Elementary
    School, Waterloo, IL

Sue McAdams, Former President of the North Texas Reading Council of the IRA,
    and Early Literacy Consultant, Dallas, TX